Chicago

BULLS

BY JIM GIGLIOTTI

Published by The Child's World®
1980 Lookout Drive • Mankato, MN 56003-1705
800-599-READ • www.childsworld.com

Cover: © Nam Y. Huh/AP Images.
Interior Photographs ©: AP Images: 9; Mark Duncan 5; Morry Gash 6;
Paul Saucya 10; Jeff Roberson 13; Matt Morton 26; Nick Wass 26. Dream-
stime.com: Jim Roberts 13. Newscom: John Biever/Sports Illustrated/Icon
SMI 17; Icon SMI 18; John McDonough/Icon SMI 22; Patrick Schneider/
KRT 29. Imagn/USA Today Sports: Erik Williams 21; Russ Isabella 25;
Mike Dinovo 26; Kamil Krzaczynski 26.

ISBN 9781503824508
LCCN 2018964189

Printed in the United States of America
PA02416

ABOUT THE AUTHOR

Jim Gigliotti has worked for the University of Southern California's athletic department, the Los Angeles Dodgers, and the National Football League. He is now an author who has written more than 100 books, mostly for young readers, on a variety of topics.

TABLE OF
CONTENTS

Go, Bulls! 4

Who Are the Bulls? 7

Where They Came From. 8

Who They Play .11

Where They Play 12

The Basketball Court 15

Good Times. .16

Tough Times .19

All the Right Moves 20

Heroes Then .23

Heroes Now .24

What They Wear 27

Team Stats 28

Glossary 30

Find Out More 31

Index 32

GO, BULLS!

The Bulls were the NBA's best team of the 1990s. They were a **dynasty**. They won the title six times. Chicago's Michael Jordan was the main reason. He was the game's biggest star. Chicago has tried to get back to the top ever since. Today's Bulls have several good, young players. Can they return the team to its glory days? Bulls fans sure hope so!

Many experts call Michael Jordan the best player of all time. He led the Bulls to six NBA titles.

Zach LaVine's athletic skills have helped the Bulls think that a return to their glory years could be coming soon.

WHO ARE THE BULLS?

The Bulls play in the NBA Central Division. That division is part of the Eastern Conference. The other teams in the Central Division are the Cleveland Cavaliers, the Detroit Pistons, the Indiana Pacers, and the Milwaukee Bucks. The Bulls have played in the Central Division since 1981. They have won the division eight times.

WHERE THEY CAME FROM

The NBA wanted to add another team for the 1967 season. The league put the new team in Chicago. The Chicago Bulls won 33 games their first year. That may not sound like a lot. However, it is the most ever won by an NBA **expansion team**. It was enough to make the **playoffs**. In fact, the Bulls usually make the playoffs. They played their 53rd season in 2019. They have been to the playoffs 35 times.

Action from 1967 shows the Bulls playing the St. Louis Hawks. Check out the players shiny satin jerseys and short shorts.

Shaquille Harrison drives to the basket against the Pistons in a Central Division battle.

The Bulls play 82 games each season. They play 41 games at home and 41 on the road. They play four games against each of the other Central Division teams. Their big **rivals** are the Pistons. The Bulls and Pistons once met in the playoffs four years in a row. The Bulls also play 36 games against other Eastern Conference teams. They play each of the teams in the Western Conference twice. Each June, the winners of the Western and Eastern Conference play each other in the NBA Finals.

The Bulls play their home games at the United Center. It opened in the 1995 season. A big statue of Michael Jordan is outside. A **mascot** named Benny the Bull entertains the fans. He is as popular as some of the team's famous players! The Bulls played at Chicago Stadium before it was replaced with the United Center. The Bulls' home is called the "Madhouse on Madison."

A statue of Michael Jordan stands outside the Bulls home arena. Inside, fans get help cheering from Benny the Bull (left).

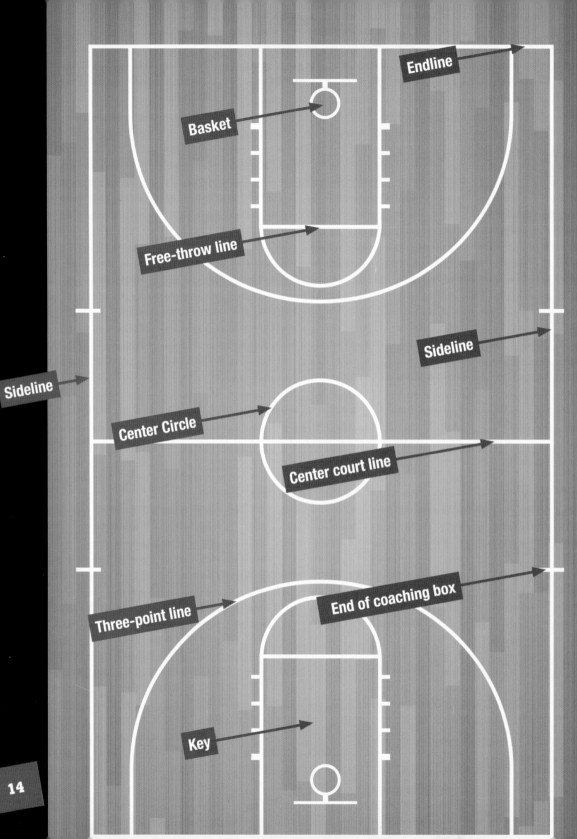

Endline

Basket

Free-throw line

Sideline

Sideline

Center Circle

Center court line

Three-point line

End of coaching box

Key

THE BASKETBALL COURT

An NBA court is 94 feet long and 50 feet wide (28.6 m by 15.24 m). Nearly all the courts are made from hard maple wood. Rubber mats under the wood help make the floor springy. Each team paints the court with its **logo** and colors. Lines on the court show the players where to take shots. The diagram on the left shows the important parts of the NBA court.

The basketball floor at the United Center is put on top of the ice surface used for hockey games. The NHL's Chicago Blackhawks play there.

GOOD TIMES

Michael Jordan had many awesome moments for the Bulls. Maybe the best came in 1998. His basket with 5.2 seconds left against Utah won the title. That was the last shot he ever took for the team. In 1993, the Bulls won their third title in a row. John Paxson hit the winning shot in the Finals. The Bulls were the first team to win 70 games in a season. They went 72–10 in 1996.

17

Michael Jordan takes one of his most famous shots ever—sending the Bulls to a win over the Utah Jazz.

Chicago's Corey Benjamin couldn't handle the ball in this 1999 game. He wasn't alone, as Chicago had one of its worst seasons.

TOUGH TIMES

The Bulls could not stop 76ers great Wilt Chamberlain in the 1968 season. In one game he made 30 of 40 shots. He scored 68 points. He grabbed 34 rebounds. The 76ers won 143–123. The Bulls' worst seasons came after Michael Jordan retired. They went 13–37 in 1999. It was their first year without him. They did not make the playoffs again until 2005.

ALL THE RIGHT MOVES

Michael Jordan could do amazing things with the basketball. He was a great dunker. He was the NBA slam-dunk champion twice. He also had a great **fadeaway** shot. Opponents could not stop it. Nobody can match MJ's moves. Current star Zach LaVine might come closest on the Bulls. He looks like MJ on drives under the basket. LaVine scoops the ball into the hoop on a reverse layup.

In basketball, a "big man" means a player who is tall and strong. It can also refer to a team's best player.

Zach LaVine rises up above his opponent for a reverse layup. He reaches past the basket to make the shot.

Scottie Pippen made it to the Hall of Fame after helping the Bulls win six titles.

HEROES THEN

Many experts call Michael Jordan the greatest player of all time. He was the Finals MVP for all six of the Bulls' titles. Scottie Pippen joined Jordan on those great teams. Jerry Sloan was a top defensive player in the team's early days. Artis Gilmore was an all-star **center**. Joakim Noah is a recent star. He helped the Bulls make the playoffs seven years in a row.

HEROES NOW

Zach LaVine became the Bulls' go-to player on offense in 2019. His scoring average went way up. Lots of Bulls get in on the action, though. The team plays at a fast pace. The Bulls are a young team. Lauri Markkanen and Wendell Carter are stars on the rise. Jabari Parker grew up in Chicago. He signed with his hometown team in the 2019 season.

Lauri Markkanen is from Finland. His homeland is cold, but his basketball skills are hot!

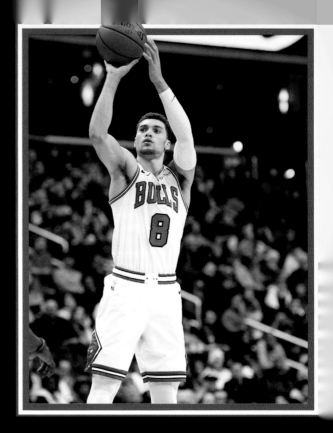

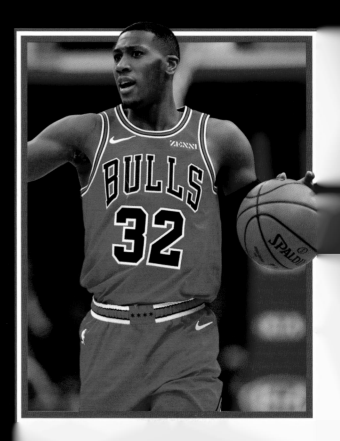

WHAT THEY WEAR

NBA players wear a **tank top** jersey. Players wear team shorts. Each player can choose his own sneakers. Some players also wear knee pads or wrist guards.

Each NBA team has more than one jersey style. The pictures at left show some of the Bulls' jerseys.

The NBA basketball is 29.5 inches (75 cm) around. It is covered with leather. The leather has small bumps called pebbles.

The pebbles on a basketball help players grip it.

TEAM STATS

Here are some of the all-time career records for the Chicago Bulls. These stats are complete through all of the 2018–19 NBA regular season.

GAMES

Michael Jordan	930
Scottie Pippen	856

REBOUNDS PER GAME

Dennis Rodman	15.3
Pau Gasol	11.4

ASSISTS PER GAME

Ennis Whatley	7.0
Norm Van Lier	6.9

FREE-THROW PCT.

George Gervin	.879
Sam Vincent	.869

STEALS PER GAME

Michael Jordan	2.5
Jerry Sloan	2.2

THREE-POINT FIELD GOALS

Kirk Hinrich	1,049
Ben Gordon	770

POINTS PER GAME

Michael Jordan	31.5
Jalen Rose	21.4

MICHAEL JORDAN

GLOSSARY

center *(SEN-ter)* a basketball position that plays near the basket

dynasty *(DY-nuh-stee)* when a team wins several championships in a row or over a period of time

expansion team *(ex-PAN-shun TEEM)* in sports, a team that is added to an existing league

fadeaway *(FAYD-uh-way)* a type of shot taken while jumping backward

logo *(LOW-go)* a team or company's symbol

mascot *(MASS-kot)* a costumed character who helps fans cheer

playoffs *(PLAY-offs)* games played between top teams to determine who moves ahead

rivals *(RY-vuhlz)* two people or groups competing for the same thing

tank top *(TANK TOP)* a style of shirt that has straps over the shoulders and no sleeves

FIND OUT MORE

IN THE LIBRARY

Bryant, Howard. *Legends: The Best Players, Games, and Teams in Basketball.* New York, NY: Philomel Books, 2016.

Doeden, Matt. *The NBA Playoffs: In Pursuit of Basketball Glory.* Minneapolis, MN: Millbrook Press, 2019.

Frisch, Nate. *The Story of the Chicago Bulls (The NBA: A History of Hoops).* Mankato, MN: Creative Paperbacks, 2015.

ON THE WEB

Visit our website for links about the Chicago Bulls:
childsworld.com/links

Note to Parents, Teachers, and Librarians: We routinely verify our Web links to make sure they are safe and active sites. So encourage your readers to check them out!

INDEX

Benjamin, Corey, 18

Benny the Bull, 12, 13

Carter, Wendell, 24

Central Division, 7, 10, 11

Chamberlain, Wilt, 19

Chicago Stadium, 12

Cleveland Cavaliers, 7

court, 15

Detroit Pistons, 7, 11

Eastern Conference, 7

Gilmore, Artis, 23

Harrison, Shaquille, 10

Indiana Pacers, 7

jerseys, 9, 27

Jordan, Michael, 4, 5, 12, 13, 16, 17, 19, 20, 23

LaVine, Zach, 6, 20, 21, 24

Markkanen, Lauri, 24, 25

Milwaukee Bucks, 7

Noah, Joakim, 23

Parker, Jabari, 24

Paxson, John, 16

Philadelphia 76ers, 19

Pippen, Scottie, 22, 23

St. Louis Hawks, 9

Sloan, Jerry, 23

United Center, 12, 13, 15

Utah Jazz, 16, 17

Western Conference, 11